A Retreat With
Our Lady of Guadalupe and Juan Diego

Querida Shaun
thank you for your
friendship and accompaniment
en cariño
Jeanette
March 1998

Other titles in the A Retreat With... *Series:*

A Retreat With
Our Lady of Guadalupe and Juan Diego

Heeding the Call

Virgilio Elizondo
&
Gloria Ines Loya
Alex Garcia-Rivera
Jeanette Rodriguez
Anita de Luna
Rosendo Urrabazo

ST. ANTHONY MESSENGER PRESS

Cincinnati, Ohio

Scripture citations are taken from the *New Revised Standard Version Bible*, copyright ©1989 by the Division of Christian Education of the National Council of Churches of Christ in the U.S.A. and used by permission.

Excerpts from *Woman Hollering Creek and Other Stories* by Sandra Cisneros, copyright ©1991 by Sandra Cisneros, are reprinted by permission of Vintage Books.

Excerpts from *The Answer/La Respuesta* by Sor Juana Ines de la Cruz, copyright ©1994 by Sor Juana Ines de la Cruz, edited and translated by E. Arenal and A. Powell, are reprinted by permission of Feminist Press.

Excerpts from *El Mensaie de Maria de Guadalupe* by Clodomiro L. Siller Acuna, copyright ©1989 by Clodomiro L. Siller Acuna, are reprinted by permission of Editorial Guadalupe.

Excerpts from *MCDP Post Autonomy Reflections* by Anita de Luna, copyright ©1994 by Anita de Luna, are reprinted by permission of MCDP Publications.

Excerpts from "Our Lady of Guadalupe to Juan Diego," CARA Studies on Popular Devotion, Volume 2: *Guadalupan Studies*, Monograph No. 6, are reprinted by permission of the publisher.

Cover illustration by Steve Erspamer, S.M.
Cover and book design by Mary Alfieri
Electronic format and pagination by Sandy L. Digman

ISBN 0-86716-323-2

Copyright ©1998, Virgilio Elizondo, Gloria Ines Loya, Alex Garcia-Rivera, Jeanette Rodriguez, Anita de Luna and Rosendo Urrabazo

Published by St. Anthony Messenger Press
Printed in the U.S.A.

Contents

Introducing A Retreat With...

Twenty years ago I made a weekend retreat at a Franciscan house on the coast of New Hampshire. The retreat director's opening talk was as lively as a long-range weather forecast. He told us how completely God loves each one of us—without benefit of lively anecdotes or fresh insights.

As the friar rambled on, my inner critic kept up a sotto voce commentary: "I've heard all this before." "Wish he'd say something new that I could chew on." "That poor man really doesn't have much to say." Ever hungry for manna yet untasted, I devalued any experience of hearing the same old thing.

After a good night's sleep, I awoke feeling as peaceful as a traveler who has at last arrived safely home. I walked across the room toward the closet. On the way I passed the sink with its small framed mirror on the wall above. Something caught my eye like an unexpected presence. I turned, saw the reflection in the mirror and said aloud, "No wonder he loves me!"

This involuntary affirmation stunned me. What or whom had I seen in the mirror? When I looked again, it was "just me," an ordinary person with a lower-than-average reservoir of self-esteem. But I knew that in the initial vision I had seen God-in-me breaking through like a sudden sunrise.

At that moment I knew what it meant to be made in the divine image. I understood right down to my size eleven feet what it meant to be loved exactly as I was. Only later did I connect this revelation with one granted to the Trappist monk-writer Thomas Merton. As he reports in *Conjectures of a Guilty Bystander*, while standing all unsuspecting on a street corner one day, he was overwhelmed by the "joy of being...a member of a race in which God Himself became incarnate.... There is no way of telling people that they are all walking around shining like the sun."

As an absentminded homemaker may leave a wedding ring on the kitchen windowsill, so I have often mislaid this precious conviction. But I have never forgotten that particular retreat. It persuaded me that the Spirit rushes in where it will. Not even a boring director or a judgmental retreatant can withstand the "violent wind" that "fills the entire house" where we dwell in expectation (see Acts 2:2).

So why deny ourselves any opportunity to come aside awhile and rest on holy ground? Why not withdraw from the daily web that keeps us muddled and wound? Wordsworth's complaint is ours as well: "The world is too much with us." There is no flu shot to protect us from infection by the skepticism of the media, the greed of commerce, the alienating influence of technology. We need retreats as the deer needs the running stream.

An Invitation

This book and its companions in the *A Retreat With...* series from St. Anthony Messenger Press are designed to meet that need. They are an invitation to choose as director some of the most powerful, appealing and wise mentors our faith tradition has to offer.

Our directors come from many countries, historical

2

eras and schools of spirituality. At times they are teamed to sing in close harmony (for example, Francis de Sales, Jane de Chantal and Aelred of Rievaulx on spiritual friendship). Others are paired to kindle an illuminating fire from the friction of their differing views (such as Augustine of Hippo and Mary Magdalene on human sexuality). All have been chosen because, in their humanness and their holiness, they can help us grow in self-knowledge, discernment of God's will and maturity in the Spirit.

Inviting us into relationship with these saints and holy ones are inspired authors from today's world, women and men whose creative gifts open our windows to the Spirit's flow. As a motto for the authors of our series, we have borrowed the advice of Dom Frederick Dunne to the young Thomas Merton. Upon joining the Trappist monks, Merton wanted to sacrifice his writing activities lest they interfere with his contemplative vocation. Dom Frederick wisely advised, "Keep on writing books that make people love the spiritual life."

That is our motto. Our purpose is to foster (or strengthen) friendships between readers and retreat directors—friendships that feed the soul with wisdom, past and present. Like the scribe "trained for the kingdom of heaven," each author brings forth from his or her storeroom "what is new and what is old" (Matthew 13:52).

The Format

The pattern for each *A Retreat With...* remains the same; readers of one will be in familiar territory when they move on to the next. Each book is organized as a seven-session retreat that readers may adapt to their own schedules or to the needs of a group.

Day One begins with an anecdotal introduction called "Getting to Know Our Directors." Readers are given a telling glimpse of the guides with whom they will be sharing the retreat experience. A second section, "Placing Our Directors in Context," will enable retreatants to see the guides in their own historical, geographical, cultural and spiritual settings.

Having made the human link between seeker and guide, the authors go on to "Introducing Our Retreat Theme." This section clarifies how the guide(s) are especially suited to explore the theme and how the retreatant's spirituality can be nourished by it.

After an original "Opening Prayer" to breathe life into the day's reflection, the author, speaking with and through the mentor(s), will begin to spin out the theme. While focusing on the guide(s)' own words and experience, the author may also draw on Scripture, tradition, literature, art, music, psychology or contemporary events to illuminate the path.

Each day's session is followed by reflection questions designed to challenge, affirm and guide the reader in integrating the theme into daily life. A "Closing Prayer" brings the session full circle and provides a spark of inspiration for the reader to harbor until the next session.

Days Two through Six begin with "Coming Together in the Spirit" and follow a format similar to Day One. Day Seven weaves the entire retreat together, encourages a continuation of the mentoring relationship and concludes with "Deepening Your Acquaintance," an envoi to live the theme by God's grace, the director(s)' guidance and the retreatant's discernment. A closing section of Resources serves as a larder from which readers may draw enriching books, videos, cassettes and films.

We hope readers will experience at least one of those memorable "No wonder God loves me!" moments. And we hope that they will have "talked back" to the mentors, as good friends are wont to do.

A case in point: There was once a famous preacher who always drew a capacity crowd to the cathedral. Whenever he spoke, an eccentric old woman sat in the front pew directly beneath the pulpit. She took every opportunity to mumble complaints and contradictions— just loud enough for the preacher to catch the drift that he was not as wonderful as he was reputed to be. Others seated down front glowered at the woman and tried to shush her. But she went right on needling the preacher to her heart's content.

When the old woman died, the congregation was astounded at the depth and sincerity of the preacher's grief. Asked why he was so bereft, he responded, "Now who will help me to grow?"

All of our mentors in *A Retreat With...* are worthy guides. Yet none would seek retreatants who simply said, "Where you lead, I will follow. You're the expert." In truth, our directors provide only half the retreat's content. Readers themselves will generate the other half.

As general editor for the retreat series, I pray that readers will, by their questions, comments, doubts and decision-making, fertilize the seeds our mentors have planted.

And may the Spirit of God rush in to give the growth.

Gloria Hutchinson
Series Editor
Conversion of Saint Paul, 1995

Getting to Know Our Directors

It happened on December 9, 1531. The place was an unimposing hill in Tepeyac, Mexico. A poor, middle-aged Indian Christian named Juan Diego was on his way to church when he was distracted from his way by the sound of beautiful music. As he sought its source, a woman's voice called him by name.

Juan Diego would never be the same. The woman identified herself as the "holy Virgin Mary, Mother of the true God." She was dressed in Indian garb covered with Aztec symbols and wearing the Aztec sash of a pregnant woman. She spoke not in Spanish, the language of the European conquerors, but in Nahuatl—Juan Diego's own tongue. Her features were those of the indigenous people, and her eyes shone with compassion.

To one like Juan Diego who had eyes to see, Mary's attire communicated powerful messages. Her rich blue mantle spoke of royalty, while the gold stars emblazoned on it signaled prophecies of a dying civilization that would soon experience new birth. The Lady's red robe indicated the blood of the indigenous people, shed so abundantly during the European conquest. She wore both a Christian cross (on her brooch) and an Aztec cross (centered on her womb). Her splendor was greater than that of the sun which framed her (a symbol of the Aztec deity).

Promising to alleviate the sufferings of the people, *la Morenita*[1] (the Little Dark One) commissions Juan Diego to carry a message to Archbishop Juan de Zumarraga. She wants a temple built in her honor on this very hill. Despite his qualms, the poor man does his Lady's bidding. The skeptical bishop insists on a sign that will authenticate Juan Diego's strange story.

Taking rejection as a proof of his own unworthiness, the messenger begs to be replaced by a more imposing personage. La Morenita is not so easily deterred. She insists that Juan Diego is her chosen disciple. Even when Juan, whose uncle Bernardino is dying, tries to avoid the Lady on his way to find a priest to prepare his uncle for death, la Morenita intervenes by miraculously healing the uncle.

To comply with the Archbishop's demand for a sign, Mary invites Juan to gather roses blooming inexplicably in December among Tepeyac's native cacti. Her disciple obeys, filling his *tilma* (a coarse cloak of cactus fiber worn knotted over one shoulder) with the lush blossoms. He presents the tilma to la Morenita. She arranges the roses to her own liking and ties the end of Juan's cloak around his neck. "This is the sign that you are to take to the lord bishop," she says, warning him not to unfold the tilma until he is in the hierarch's presence.

When Juan follows these instructions, the roses tumble out of his tilma at the archbishop's feet. And on the cloak itself is imprinted a beautiful image of la Morenita herself in an attitude of prayer. That same tilma is today enshrined in the Basilica of Our Lady of Guadalupe at the foot of Tepeyac in Mexico City. It is six-and-a-half feet long and over three feet wide. The sight of that image is said to have motivated the conversion of eight million Indians during the seven years following its appearance.

The name *Guadalupe* arose through a Spanish mistranslation of a Nahuatl word used by Mary in addressing Juan Bernardino as she healed him. Guadalupe is translated "the one who crushes the head of the serpent" (possibly referring to the stone serpent, an Aztec idol). The name also refers to a Spanish village where a statue of the Virgin had been discovered two hundred years earlier.

In 1754 Pope Benedict XIV made December 12 the Feast of Our Lady of Guadalupe, saying "No other nation has been so favored." In 1910 Pope Pius X declared her the patroness of Latin America. And thirty-five years later Our Lady of Guadalupe's patronage was extended throughout the Americas by Pope Pius XII. Juan Diego himself was beatified in 1990 by Pope John Paul II, who in 1997 at the Synod for America described Our Lady of Guadalupe as the "star of the first and new evangelization of America."

The Basilica of Our Lady of Guadalupe continues to draw millions of pilgrims each year. Miraculous healings and conversions are regularly attributed to la Morenita who is seen as the special advocate of the poor with whom she identified herself. Her intercessory power has sustained them through oppression and war, economic injustice and, at times, the failure of the Church to heed their cries.

Placing Our Directors in Context

The event at Tepeyac occurred only twelve years after the conquest of the Aztecs by Hernando Cortez. With ruthless single-mindedness, the Spanish wiped out a highly developed civilization and deprived them of their ancestral gods. Understandably, the indigenous people did not take kindly to the God of the Christians preached by Franciscan missionaries. Many believed that their existence as a people had come to an end.

Undeterred by doubts about the rightness of their

cause, the conquistadores conveyed the image of a machismo God bent on judging and punishing those who resisted the Christian faith. They believed that God had sent them to convert the heathen and stamp out idolatry. While the missionaries preached a God "who so loved the world that he gave his only-begotten Son," they were seen as representatives of a merciless civilization. Only a minority of the indigenous people accepted this foreign religion from across the sea.

Not until the appearance of la Morenita did the majority see the true face of Christianity. Mary, singer of the Magnificat, prophet of the Lord who "has cast down the mighty from their thrones and sent the rich away empty-handed," revealed both a loving God and the God-given dignity of the Indian people.

Her coming marks the turning point in the sixteenth-century history of Latin America.

Notes

[1] The use of Spanish diminutives—*ita* or *ito*, as in *la Morenita* or *Juanito*—can be translated as either "little" or "dear." Both usages appear in this book.

DAY ONE
Emerging From Darkness

Introducing Our Retreat Theme

Do you want God to transform the sadness of your life into a new joy? Do you want God to change your nightmares into sweet dreams? Do you want God to bring meaning out of the apparently senseless situations of life? Do you want God to put new energy into your tired life? If so, join us for a fascinating adventure into the graciousness of God's love which comes to us in totally unexpected ways.

Welcome to one of the greatest experiences of personal transformation ever recounted in the Americas. It is truly the beginning of new life. We invite you to make this transforming experience your own. As you walk with Juan Diego, reexperience your own moments of chaos, desperation and darkness as the moments of greatest fecundity. See how God interrupts your own plans and routines to bring about new life. Rejoice as your darkest breakdowns become your greatest breakthroughs. Juan Diego will be our guide.

We usually do not understand why God allows disasters and disappointments in our lives. We would like a heavenly peace here on earth, but we know that is simply not realistic. Job certainly did not understand his chaotic life. I am sure that Mary struggled to understand the condemnation and execution of Jesus. This sorrow is a thread that binds all human experience. Juan Diego will help us to see how moments of darkness are but the beginning of new life.

I had a sense of this when I first decided to prepare for the priesthood. My father was a holy man, but, like many Latin Americans, he didn't believe in priests. I knew my decision would disappoint him terribly, but I couldn't turn my back on God. I prayed, pondered, put it off for a while and finally gathered the courage to tell him. It was the hardest thing I have ever done. As I expected, our family harmony fell apart. It took several years to reestablish that harmony, but eventually we were able to rejoice together in my new existence as an ordained priest. Throughout that difficult time of darkness, it was Our Lady of Guadalupe who gave me the strength to continue forward on what was often an uncertain path.

I hope you will find our retreat with Juan Diego and Our Lady of Guadalupe as spiritually enriching as we have. All of us who worked on this retreat have known the beautiful, transforming and life-giving power of Our Lady of Guadalupe through the experience of Juan Diego. We are: Jeanette Rodriguez, a theological professor, wife and mother who has heard many testimonies of Guadalupe from ordinary people; Rosendo Urrabazo, a Claretian priest and a pastoral counselor, who has studied the psyche of Mexican American men; Gloria Loya, a religious woman who has worked in the pastoral fields of California all her life; Alex Garcia-Rivera, a convert to Catholicism, author, professor of theology, husband and father; Anita de Luna, former superior general of a religious congregation dedicated to Our Lady of Guadalupe, who has devoted her whole life to working with people at the grassroots level. I am a diocesan priest with thirty-three years in parish work; much of that time has been dedicated to understanding and promoting devotion to God's greatest gift to the Americas: Our Lady of Guadalupe. We are all pastoral workers involved with people in the everyday struggles of life; but essentially we are like you: ordinary human beings, Christians.

The wealth of this retreat is not only the richness of the subject matter, but also the diversity of the authors who have contributed to it. Each of us has experienced Our Lady of Guadalupe and Juan Diego in a special way, and we look forward to sharing these life-giving experiences with you.

We invite you to find moments in your life's journey similar to those of Juan Diego. Let yourself discover in the unexpected interruptions of your plans and agendas the loving, healing and saving power of God through Our Lady of Guadalupe. A special and precious gift of God, she comes precisely at our greatest moments of need. She comes to us all without exception. That is her message and her gift. From the arrival of the new people in the Americas, she proclaimed herself to be the mother of all the inhabitants of this land, saying to us as to Juan Diego: "You need not be afraid, am I not here!"

Opening Prayer

O Mother of God and our mother, you are the great light from heaven which illuminated the darkness of Juan Diego during the darkest night of his soul, transforming his agony into the joy of new life. Come to me during this retreat so that your maternal presence may be as enlightening of my darkness and as healing of my wounds as it was for Juan Diego.

As I meet you and converse with you through the

person of Juan Diego, let me encounter your tenderness, your kindness, your compassion, your joy and the strength of new life which has been your gift throughout the ages and which will be your gift to me today.

Come, O Virgin of Guadalupe, and make your abode in me. Make of me another temple where you show your love and compassion to all the inhabitants of this land. Amen.

RETREAT SESSION ONE

My name is Juan Diego. I was born and raised in the land of the eagles who are the great mediators between heaven and earth. In 1531, I live in the beautiful valley of Mexico City surrounded by its two snow-covered sentinels: Popocatepetl and Ixtahihuatl which reach out from the depths of the earth to the heights of heaven. I work hard tilling the soil and live a simple but peaceful life with my family—grandparents and uncles and aunts—and a few animals and beautiful flowers. I love the sunrise which is always accompanied by the singing of the birds. There seem to be as many kinds of birds as the stars in the sky. When the rain comes, it is quiet and nourishing; the sunshine is always warm and radiant. Clouds of many shapes move against the blue sky to remind us of our own brief journey of life: here one moment, gone the next. Life is like a dream, our ancestors told us, and we have no reason to doubt that at death we will awake. The God of the near and the far away keeps us alive, and there is never a moment when I am not aware of God's presence. How could earth with its valleys and mountains, its lakes and rivers, its flowers and trees, its vegetables and fruits,

its animals and people, be so beautiful if God is not beauty itself?

But I also know that life is not always beautiful. I know that back in 1519, something happened that stripped everything of meaning, beauty and harmony. Suddenly my whole beautiful world fell apart! Has that ever happened to you? I am sure it has. For in reality it happens to all of us. This is life.

In that year, foreign men on horses came rushing into our world. (We had never even seen horses. We did not know what they were.) Their weapons could kill at a distance—they seemed magical. The men destroyed our cities, devastated our way of life, burned our temples and shops. The priests who came with them told us our gods were false.

Darkness and chaos became our daily lot. Tears and lamentations replaced our dances and songs of joy. The sun no longer seemed to give life, and stars appeared only as reminders of a distant past when everything made sense.

All of a sudden everything went sour! There was no one to turn to. Everyone was telling us what to do, but no one was listening to us, no one even tried to understand our pain and misery. Isn't this the greatest suffering in your life also, when there is no one around to share your pain, to accompany you in your suffering and sorrow? The new priests said they wanted to save us, but we really could not understand for what. Nothing made sense anymore!

Our tears flowed like a rushing stream after a downpour, but there was no one to see them or dry them for us; our cry shrilled through the air like a wild animal wounded in the hunt, but there was no one who was willing to listen to us. Silence became our lot, our faces became empty of expression, our bodies seemed to move around without a soul. I know that you have had times of devastation. That is why I invite you to walk with me because I want to walk with you, I want to accompany you, I want to share your sorrow and pain, that my own sorrow and pain might become a source of healing to you.

The new priests, the ones with the Christian religion, were kind. They wore the clothes of poor men, yet they were honored by the rich and powerful hidalgos who now ruled our land. We learned to trust and respect these holy men, even though they were so different from us. As they spoke about the creation of the universe, how out of the chaos and darkness God had created everything, I was reminded of our own ancient teachings of how in the midst of chaos and darkness the gods had liberated and brought about a new creation. I realize now that, even as we listened in our own darkness and chaos, a new creation was being prepared and was about to come into being.

Our new priests also told us about a great ancient empire—the Roman Empire—that conquered many lands and peoples. It was in one of those tiny, subjected lands that the Son of God was born in the dark and sacred stillness, to bring the peace and love of God to all people. They told us that, though the powerful tortured and cruelly killed him, though he seemed abandoned even by God, he was resurrected, brought to life again. That moment of supreme darkness brought forth the moment of God's greatest glory.

This was a wonderful story and I grew to believe it. Yet there was still something missing. Something in the depths of my heart. I am sure you have heard beautiful words. You like what you hear, you agree, you find it exciting and yet it doesn't seem to touch you. Well, that is how I felt. But I invite you to continue with me, because God is always greater than the best of men and women.

I left home early one morning while it was still dark,

not only in the sky but in the pain and confusion in my soul. I was headed for church to learn more about God. I was thinking about the wisdom of my ancestors who seemed to understand the creative power of darkness and about the teaching of the new priests: While it was still dark, God had created life; while it was still dark, God had become human for us; while it was still dark, the Son of God had burst from the tomb in the fullness of life. Yes, I was confused and in pain and spiritual darkness, but as I walked, I knew something was happening within that darkness. Something was stirring that I could not quite identify. It was a restlessness, an anxiety, a feeling that something—I didn't know what—would happen.

The ways of God are so far beyond us. I see things in terms of the here and now, and often I think what is happening is horrible and senseless. God sees from the heavens the whole continuum of life and sees how even those things that appear to be terrible are but preparatory moments for something new and fascinating. God is good beyond our wildest imaginings.

As I walked through the mesquites and the nopales, I kicked the sand and looked at the stars, smelled the various aromas of the plants around me. I kept asking myself: Why all this darkness and confusion? Is this the end of all our happiness, or is God going to offer us something new? If there is a God, and I believed there was, there must be some good purpose to all of our troubles. This is what I believed, but I felt very differently, very empty.

I am sure that you, my friend, companion and fellow walker, have had similar situations in your life—an unexpected divorce, a terminal illness, a child of yours condemned to prison, the loss of a job, the betrayal of a friend. There are so many times when our whole world falls apart, when darkness invades us.

17

One of our companions—a man who lives in your time—had such a trial. He had always worked for the same company. He took his job very seriously; it was the most dominant, consistent thing in his life. One morning, he reported to work and was told that his department, and his job, were gone—eliminated from the company's budget. His work was excellent, they said, but no longer necessary. He was fifty-four and his training very specialized; he had no prospects for another job. His career was finished. But that was just the beginning of the tragedy. He started to feel guilty, as if he had brought this misfortune upon himself, though he knew he didn't. He felt ashamed and embarrassed. He didn't want to visit friends or do things he used to do. He lost interest in almost everything; he felt as if his identity had vanished along with his income. His only concern was how he and his family would survive. The corporate buyouts of the modern business world had crashed into his life the way the conquistadores had come crashing into the life of my people many years before. His life, like mine, was suddenly devastated. What can God want in all this?

Sadly, these moments of destruction happen to everyone. No one can avoid them forever. Even those lucky enough to escape personal tragedy must witness it in others; the death of a loved one brings us the experience of emptiness and finality. As we begin to reflect on this retreat, I invite you to not run away from these moments, do not try to avoid them or escape them. Don't go looking for them—they will come on their own all too quickly. But when they do come, don't let them destroy you or your life. It is hard to believe when you are suffering, but our moments of supreme pain and darkness are the moments of our greatest potential; they are the moments when the power of God reaches the depths of our being to touch us, heal us and start us on a new path.

It is in the darkest moments of life that we must receive the Spirit, allowing God to recreate us and our world.

For Reflection

- *In what ways have you experienced the kind of darkness Juan Diego describes? How did it change you?*

- *Juan speaks of the inadequacy of religious teachings that did not "reach the depths of my heart and soul." Have there been times when you felt this way about the teachings of your own faith? How did God reach you in the depths of your soul?*

- *What proof can you offer from your own life (or that of another) that our times of darkness "are the moments of our greatest potential"? Describe one such experience to someone who may need to hear it. Or, write it in your journal where it will be available when needed.*

Closing Prayer

O Blessed Juan Diego, as I begin this retreat with you as my guide, I ask that you accompany me not only during these days, but during the entire journey of my life. You were on the way to hear and learn about God and in the process you experienced the Divine Presence through Our Lady of Guadalupe. Help me to equally experience the Divine Presence in my life, transforming my darkness into the brightness of a new day. Walk with me through any and all obstacles so that God will imprint the divine image upon my heart and soul. Amen.

GLORIA INES LOYA, P.B.V.M.

DAY TWO
Breaking the Routine

Coming Together in the Spirit

The story of Guadalupe as a source for our spirituality and prayer is embedded in the hearts and collective memory of the people of the Americas. Many Hispanic families have immigrated from Latin America to the United States carrying the image of Guadalupe in their hearts or discovering it anew after living in the United States. Her image and presence have grown profoundly as a sign of hope and faith for thousands of families.

Members of the Rodriquez family tell how they left Mexico in the 1920's when their father was killed during the Mexican Revolution. Their mother, a young widow, had to leave her homeland with seven children in order to find safety. Left alone with the care of her children, she had no time to mourn the death of her husband. She brought them to *el norte* (the north) to find work and a new home, finding strength in prayer and hope in Our Lady of Guadalupe.

As her children grew they, too, learned to trust in Our Lady of Guadalupe. They recall how they were awakened at dawn on her feast day to dress and prepare to join in the parish procession and fiesta in her honor. Now adults, they remember the sweet smell of chocolate and *pan dulce*

(Mexican bread) shared by all after the singing of the *mañanitas* (first light songs) at dawn. On those cold, dark winter mornings there was a strong sense of family and community as everyone lifted up their hearts and voices in praising la Morenita (the Little Dark One).

As young adults, two members of the Rodriquez family were profoundly moved when, during the 1970's, members of the farm workers' movement lifted up banners carrying the image of Guadalupe in their processions; it was a reminder that the struggle of the Hispanic people for justice was based on a great respect and love for la Morenita. A spiritual quality marked that struggle for compassion. The image of la Morenita inspired prayer and peace in everyone in that conflict, even during the most frustrating, confusing and potentially violent moments. Her presence has sustained faithful families through tremendous difficulties.

Defining Our Thematic Context

What image of Mary do you carry from your past? How was she a part of your family history? What is the figure of Mary that you hold most dear now? The Rodriquez family has carried the figure of Maria of Guadalupe in their memories, and she has been a sign of grace for them in transforming darkness into a new dawn of hope. By taking time to reflect on the Guadalupe story, we, too, can find new paths of grace and the courage to break with the routine, and meet the challenges that confront us.

During this day of prayer with Our Lady of Guadalupe, we will focus on her invitation to Juan Diego to help his people overcome the obstacles created by the dramatic social and political changes of the time. We will consider how Juan had to change his own point of view before he could become a catalyst for the belief and conversion of millions.

Opening Prayer

I pray to you, Virgen Maria de Guadalupe, la Morenita, lead me as you did Juan Diego. Open my heavy heart to the guidance and inspiration of the Spirit who invites me to become your friend by striving to live the gospel message. Show me how to escape this stagnation, break this routine, and overcome the barriers that often make me unable to receive your guidance. Give me the grace to hear your message and the courage to bring it to others.

RETREAT SESSION TWO

In the middle of winter, in the darkness of the early morning, Juan Diego is stunned by his encounter with the sacred image of Guadalupe. The experience is one of intellectual and emotional dissonance and confusion. Why is this so?

Juan Diego represents all who have been conquered during the European invasion of the Americas. He is keenly aware of all the suffering and death brought on by the conquest of the indigenous people of Mexico. Yet, on this morning he is on his way to the house of God to continue learning about the Christian message from the official ministers of the Church.

As he listens to the beautiful music surrounding the hillside of Tepeyac, he hears the voice calling to him. He slowly begins to see, to hear and to comprehend. As the Guadalupe event unfolds, it is clear that Juan Diego represents the world of the suffering; he continues to face powerful forces that keep him from accepting the woman's word of life. The greatest obstructions facing Juan Diego are:

- poverty
- the subjugation of his people
- his adoption of the faith of the conquistadores
- his intermediary role between two worldviews and two spiritualities.

Let's examine each of these obstacles and see how we can identify with Juan Diego.

1. Poverty

With the coming of the Spaniards to Mexico in 1519, the cultural destruction of the new world took place. The time for the old mythologies and rituals of the ancient Mexicans ended suddenly. This culture shock experienced by the indigenous people affected their laws and language, religion and calendar, social status and even their health. The great city of Tenochtitlán, with its magnificent pyramids, irrigation systems and ingenious farming methods became Mexico City, the capital of New Spain. The Europeans' disrespect for the natives' traditions, contempt for their ancient spirituality, and superior military force was debilitating. The darkness of a tragic economic and social poverty began in the Americas, and this poverty was experienced by Juan Diego.

We debate so much about the poor in our society that we can hardly communicate on this issue, let alone bring it into our prayer and Christian living. Juan Diego represents not only the poverty experienced by his people after the conquest, but also *our* poverty. Our poverty may not be as radical as his, but we may experience the loss of a job, security, medical benefits, an accustomed place in society. We see the homeless and hungry on our city streets, knowing how easily we could be among them. Like Juan Diego, we must hear the cries of the poor in this insecure and chaotic world as if they were our own.

> ...for I was hungry and you gave me no food. I was thirsty and you gave me nothing to drink, I was a stranger and you did not welcome me, naked and you did not give me clothing, sick and in prison, and you did not visit me. Then they will also answer, "Lord, when was it that we saw you hungry or thirsty or a stranger or naked or sick or in prison, and did not take care of you?" Then he will answer them, "Truly I tell you, just as you did not do it to one of the least of these, you did not do it to me."[1]

2. The Subjugation of His People

> My dear lady...I understood perfectly the (bishop's) response. He thinks that maybe this is my invention that you want a new church built here.... My lady, you have sent me into a place that I do not belong and where I should not walk or stand.[2]

Juan Diego was called by Our Lady to proclaim a message that holds the word of God for all, even for the official authorities of the ecclesial and European worlds. By choosing a native as her ambassador, she forces Juan and those to whom he speaks to see all the indigenous people as they are esteemed by God. Juan must transcend his social position to go into the stronghold of the dominant culture and its highest authorities. He knows they will not accept him or his message. In their eyes, he has no credibility, no credentials. Most challengingly, he doubts his own worthiness, perhaps even his sanity.

The story of Guadalupe reminds us to reflect on how Juan Diego's rejection is mirrored by the treatment of the marginalized in our society. As a faith community, we must commit ourselves to remove all barriers to equality in employment, housing and education. As we learn to appreciate the importance of the message delivered by Juan Diego, we should understand that all people deserve to be listened to and respected.

> Sor Juana Ines de la Cruz of Mexico was a brilliant religious woman. Sor Juana's prodigious talent, furthered by intense efforts that began in early childhood, produced a serious intellectual while she was still in her teens. She taught herself the forms of classical rhetoric and the language of law, theology, and literature. At every turn, from her courtly and learned yet marginalized standpoint, she contradicted—or deconstructed—artistic, intellectual, and religious views that would refuse her and others like her the right to express themselves.[3]

3. His Adoption of the Faith of the Conquistadores

> My lady I must arrive at your house in Mexico, Tlatelolco, to continue learning about the divine things that are given and taught by our priests, the delegates of our Lord.[4]

While Juan Diego represents the indigenous world and all who have been rejected by the powerful, he is also rejected by his own people. In the beginning of the story he is on his way to Tlatelolco, the site of the first Christian cathedral in Mexico. The cathedral and Juan Diego become signs of the new faith, both of which are paradoxical for the indigenous people. We can imagine his people questioning the validity of what the missionaries preach—they proclaim a God of love, but the native civilization was overcome by violence. They must think of Juan Diego as a traitor for forsaking the traditional ways. And then for him to be called to represent the Blessed Virgin so honored by the Europeans! Many of the natives are still worshipping their traditional gods while the missionaries make efforts to evangelize them. Some may think it prudent to pretend to believe the religion being forced upon them. But to be even more daring in this new faith than the missionaries must seem suspicious.

But as Juan Diego convinces the Europeans of the truth of his story, his own people are convinced, too. The wondrous image of Our Lady of Guadalupe and her choice of ambassador demonstrate to them that the Christian faith is not a possession of the invaders but a gift to all who have the courage to accept it. Their dark night of suffering brings a dawn of great faith.

Listen to a woman who, like Juan, has discovered la Morenita's power—and her own:

> *Virgencita* (Little Virgin)....I don't know how it all fell in place. That you could have the power to rally a people when a country was born, and again during the civil war, and during a farm workers' strike in California made me think maybe there is power in my mother's patience, strength in my grandmother's endurance. Because those who suffer have a special power, don't they? The power of understanding someone else's pain. And understanding is the beginning of healing.[5]

4. His Intermediary Role Between Two Worldviews and Two Spiritualities

Through the Guadalupe story we see that Juan Diego faces the same burdens many of us do today, and more. He represents all of us struggling to know the way to God.

He is one of the poor and oppressed who has known darkness and death. He does not belong to the culture of power. While he is learning about the Christian faith, his own people look at him with distrust and scorn.

As Juan receives his commission, he experiences a wide range of feelings, of impulses and dichotomies. He is in the middle of two contradictory social, religious and cultural worlds. He asks himself, "If this is of God, why am I in such inner conflict and turmoil?" After all, he was on his way to church, he was doing the right thing. Why has he been called rather than one more worthy, or at least more credible? His people had been suffering since the conquest. Why must even deeper desolation be brought upon him?

Juan Diego is much like the psalmist who cries out for mercy and compassion for himself and for his people while waiting for the dark night to become a new dawn.

> I wait for the LORD, my soul waits,
> and in his word I hope;
> my soul waits for the Lord
> more than those who watch for the morning,
> more than those who watch for the morning.[6]

The new day begins to appear as Juan Diego accepts and embraces the call of discipleship. This requires of him, as of us, great discernment in sifting through his feelings of surprise and of confusion as he passes over the sacred hill of Tepeyac. He finally sees that he is being asked to break with all his routines, all his traditions, by becoming a messenger not only to his own community, but to the conquistadores and all those who would someday inhabit the Americas. With the patient and firm presence of Our Lady of Guadalupe, Juan Diego bridges two worlds.

On the desertic hill of Tepeyac, beautiful sounds beckon each of us to become partners in proclaiming the word of God in the Americas. Through the message of Guadalupe and Juan Diego's struggle, God's grace has been offered to each of us. Through it, we can find the strength to live in the darkness, keeping faith in the dawn.

For Reflection

- *How have you experienced poverty in your life?*

- *How do you welcome those who are poor, strangers or foreigners into your world?*

- *In what ways have you experienced rejection? Have you promoted dignity and acceptance for others by insisting that their voices be heard? How can you welcome all people as part of the fabric of a rich, diverse society and as the children of God?*

- *How do you feel when you sense that God is calling you? Does this invitation cause disruption or confusion for you, your community or your friends? Have you trusted that God is always faithful, offering you a deeper life?*

Closing Prayer

Juan Diego, faithful disciple of the Patroness of the Americas and my brother, I ask that you accompany me in listening for the invitation God offers me. Pray that I will have your strength and faith in overcoming those obstacles that keep me from hearing and obeying the voice of God. Help me have the courage to break with the routine. In times of darkness, teach me to persevere. Give me your steadfast endurance in proclaiming the reign of mercy, compassion and justice in the Americas.

Notes

1 Matthew 25:42-45.

2 The Nican mopohua document, written in Nahuatl by Antonio Valeriano. Published by Luis Lazo de la Vega. Translation from Spanish by G. Loya, p. 6.

3 Sor Juana Inés de la Cruz, *The Answer/La Respuesta*, ed. and trans. E. Arenal and A. Powell (New York: Feminist Press, 1994), p. 1.

4 Nican mopohua, p. 3.

5 Sandra Cisneros, *Woman Hollering Creek and Other Stories* (New York: Vintage Books, 1991), p. 128.

6 Psalm 130:5-6.

ALEX GARCIA-RIVERA

Day Three
Finding the Secret Garden

Coming Together in the Spirit

I will never forget a certain Christmas story. Before becoming Roman Catholic, I was a Lutheran pastor beginning a mission church with Hispanics in Allentown, Pennsylvania. These folks were dirt poor. They had tried to leave the impossible conditions of the barrios of New York City only to find themselves living in housing projects under the same conditions. They lived continually on the edge of death and tragedy. My first week in Allentown—indeed, my first act as a new pastor—was to bury a two-month-old infant girl. The parents could not afford a crib, and the little girl had suffocated as she slept between her mother and father in their bed.

The mission to the Hispanic community began with the generosity of a fairly established Lutheran church in the city which had offered its facilities and worship space. Our little community began our first year by worshipping in a small chapel above the main space of the church. On our first Christmas, I gave the leaders a little money to go and buy a tree with all the trimmings for our chapel. Below, the largely Pennsylvania Dutch Lutheran community was doing the same.

During the next couple of weeks, our respective

communities both began setting up their Christmas trees. Considering the amount they had to spend, I thought our folks had done rather well. They had bought a six-foot artificial tree. When they had finished decorating, the effect was striking. The tree had been transformed into a multicolored extravaganza. Colored lights sprouted everywhere blinking a joyous beat to a silent melody. Sparks of red, yellow, blue, orange and green reflected from generous doses of tinsel "icicles" draped like Spanish moss on the branches. Everywhere hung bubbles of glass in an indescribable variety of shades, shapes and sizes. On top was their prized possession—a large rotating ball that swept the chapel in swaths of colored light.

Below, a different Christmas was imagined. The Dutch had bought an impressive tree, close to twenty feet high, cut from the Pocono forests nearby. They had adorned it with yards of unblinking white lights, strung like an elegant pearl necklace around the neck of a beautiful woman. Then, they had hung "chrismons," symbolic cutouts adorned with golden paint or buttons. The Chi-Rho, a dove, a crown and globe and various other chrismonic symbols were hung about the limbs of the giant blue-green spruce exuding a quiet dignity.

Each community peeked now and then to see what the other was doing. I will never forget their first impressions of each other's Christmas tree. The Dutch who saw the exuberance of our Christmas vision gasped in disbelief and exclaimed, "How gaudy! How vulgar!" The Puerto Ricans peering into the church below were equally astonished: "How cold! How lifeless!"

Perhaps at no other time are our Christian religious imaginations so exposed as in our celebration of Christmas. And in the United States, nowhere are they so evident as in our decoration of the Christmas tree. Here the light of our imagination reveals the life of our imagination. They merge on the green of the Christmas tree revealing a secret garden, a secret place in our souls. From this garden, we cut the blossoms of our devotion and place them as offerings to the One who made us. Thus, it surprises us to find others who obviously have visited the same garden yet have chosen different flowers to offer. The experience is as old as the story of Cain and Abel.

Defining Our Thematic Context

Juan Diego lived in a time when the clash of different offerings was unavoidable and deadly. The European expression of the Christian Church had collided with the that of the indigenous people of the Americas. It was a crisis (for both sides) between life and light—between the life of a people and the light that sustains it. Indeed, Juan Diego's fateful encounter with Our Lady of Guadalupe begins at the first light of day, the light upon which life depends.

Most of us do not perceive dawn as such a crisis. The sun always comes up tomorrow. Yet every religious imagination knows better. Sunrise is an exquisitely religious moment. Our hearts are moved whenever we experience it. This is more than a reaction to beauty; it is a response to a memory—an ancient memory of a time when dawn was not a certainty. The first light of every day is also the memory of the first light of the first day. And it is within that light that we find the creative, restless Spirit exploding in the world with new life of unimaginable diversity and color. The secret gardens of our souls are to be found within this creative light. They can no more be uniform than the life that emerged from the first light of creation.

In 1519, in a violent encounter of cultures, the conquistadores land in the Americas, conquering and devaluing the indigenous people. Each side is unable to appreciate the religious imagination—the secret garden—of the other. The missionaries scoff at Indian "superstition" and the natives mistrust men who preach peace but bring violence. Knowing this, Our Lady brings Juan Diego on a living path of rediscovery, to find again the source of all gardens, the place where light and life meet, the place of our first parents, the first garden.

This story of light and life has impact beyond its simple telling. Our Lady's garden becomes for the people of Mechica a new understanding of themselves as the people of Mexico. Since Juan Diego, generation after generation of Americans will enter the creative light of the garden of Guadalupe to find new life. Every true spiritual act is an act of rediscovery. The story of Juan Diego and Our Lady of Guadalupe can be our guide to this new life, to the secret garden in our souls.

Opening Prayer

Dear Lady, seek me out as you did Juan Diego. Call me to your garden that I may find my own. The paths I have taken in my life have left me confused and disoriented. Take me to that place where light leads to life, a life that takes me ever closer to the living God. Give me the heart of Juan Diego, so simple and pure, that I, too, may be stopped from my everyday routine to begin the journey to the first day where I will find myself. I ask, Mother of Life, in the name of the One you bear in your womb: Let me be reborn again.

Retreat Session Three

Juan Diego speaks, sharing his living memory with us:

The song catches my attention. I have been hurrying, as every Saturday morning for the past two years; catechism class begins early and it is a long way into town. Ordinarily, I would not have noticed a bird song so early in the morning. In the twilight of the dawn, the body and the mind yet sleep. Yet there is something unexpected about this melody, a sweetness so profound I cannot resist. Enchanted, I stop and listen. The music continues and my heart soars. As the sun slowly rises, it occurs to me that I have not stopped for the song; the song has stopped me. My weekly routine has been broken and I begin to sense that I am being called to a higher place, a place above the road, the top of the hill.

I hesitate. Where my heart wants to go is an old place, a sacred place. No one has gone there for years and I am not sure I should go. Some priests have told me the devil lives there, angry because the ancient wicked ways were no longer being practiced. Some of the old folks tell me it is haunted by the ghosts of our great-grandfathers and great-grandmothers—brokenhearted, even in death, over the loss of the old ways. I hesitate, the sweetness of the song confusing me, coaxing me up above, where great evil was done and ancient memories threatened. But I am caught up, outside myself. My heart decides, and I begin the journey upwards.

As I climb, the soft light of the dawn mixes with the hard darkness of the previous night. I walk through transfigured brambles and bushes. The mix of dawn and night redraw their features, and I begin to enter a secret garden. How many times have I walked through here! How familiar my knowing! Yet now in the glow of the yet-to-rise sun, what had been familiar has become a discovery. And I am beside myself. My heart responds to the enchantment of this secret place, and I long to linger in its sweetness.

Suddenly, the song ceases. All is still. The silence outside begins to enter my soul, and I, too, become still. I am one with the garden in its quiet, a quiet that is more than the absence of sound. The stillness of my soul is a lack of stiffness. I've become pliant, ready to be formed again, to sprout forth like a seed bursting into life. And like the first word of creation, I hear my name. "Juanito, Juan Dieguito!" Then I see her.

Not a devil or a ghost, Sweet Beauty smiles at me. She stands on the bramble, now filled with emerald leaves, and the turquoise sky and golden stars wrap around her like a mantle. I know she is the source of sweetness in this garden.

I ask, "Where am I?"

"Look for yourself, Juanito, what do you see?"

I look around, perhaps for the first time since I heard that beautiful bird song. All around me I sense both the familiar and the strange. I see the brambles, the twisted bushes struggling for survival, the desert landscape so familiar to these parts. Yet the twilight sun has made the familiar unfamiliar, or, rather, has made me see the familiar in unexpected ways. And about this Lady, brambles barely alive now splash the gloom with green as if they were filled with the essence of life itself.

"My sweet Lady, I see the jewels amid the sand, I see color brightening the dark, and I see what was old and familiar to me now become young and new. I am in a secret garden somehow known to me, yet surprising me. I am where I always want to be yet know I cannot stay here for long. Where am I, dear beautiful Lady?"

"You are where life and light meet, Juanito."

36

"Where is that, my Sovereign Maiden?"

"What have you learned about the Holy One, the Maker of life and light?"

"They have taught me, dear Lady, about the One who made us, who took mud out of the ground and blew life into the first Grandparent."

"Are you his grandson?"

"Oh yes, Señora, I am. We all are."

"Look again, Juanito, this is your first grandparent's place."

My heart leaps with joy and wonder. I am in the land of the first grandparents! No wonder it seems familiar and strange at the same time. Yet I have doubts. How can this be? Why did the priests come here? Did they not come from the first grandparent's place to tell us about it? Did they not come across the sea to teach us? She must know what I am thinking.

"My dear Dieguito ["little Diego"], don't be puzzled. The priests have come because the Holy One has sent them. They, too, have longed to find the first grandparent's place. Many, like you, shall also find it. Dear Juanito, don't you know who I am? I am your new Grandmother. I am your *Abuelita* (Little Grandmother), la Nueva Eva."

Again, her words catch me by surprise—la Nueva Eva, the New Eve. The first grandmother had been called Eva, the mother of life. The words of the Holy Book the priests read to us fill my heart:

> He drove out the man; and at the east of the garden
> of Eden he placed the cherubim, and a sword
> flaming and turning to guard the way to the tree of
> life.... The man named his wife Eve, because she was
> the mother of all living.[1]

As I hold these words in my heart, I hear her call my name.

"Juanito, I am the mother of all the living, I am the mother of the Living God."

"Mother of Life, can I stay here with you forever?"

"My lovely Dieguito, someday you shall, but you must tell others about the garden and their Abuelita."

"Oh Señora, I cannot bear to leave. It is so beautiful here, so soothing. My heart will break."

"Juanito, the garden will always be here. My Son has made it so. Anyone who wishes to return to the garden may do so. They only have to go to that place where life and light meet."

"But, Abuelita, how can one go to the dawn?"

"Juan, my Juanito, the dawn you carry within you. Dawn comes to the heart as well as to the fields. Light gives life not only to the creatures of the earth but also to your soul. But first light is more than the dawn of every day. It is the dawn of the first day."

I remember more words from the Holy Book:

> In the beginning when God created the heavens and the earth, the earth was a formless void and darkness covered the face of the deep, while a wind from God swept over the face of the waters. Then God said, "Let there be light"; and there was light. And God saw that the light was good; and God separated the light from the darkness. God called the light Day, and the darkness he called Night. And there was evening and there was morning, the first day.[2]

"That's right, Juanito, the first light of the first day, that's where you'll find the garden."

I look around. The garden is still here, bathed in the softness of this dawn's light. Somehow I understand what she is saying. I know she is simply describing a world present to me. Yet I stumble about the reasonings of my mind and heart. How can this be? How can one go back to the first day? How can one go back in time? She smiles patiently, knowingly. I realize she is not simply telling me something I should know. She is teaching me, educating me, but not like the teaching at catechism class. She is teaching me to see, to look in order to understand.

"Dear Dieguito," she continues, "without light there is no life, either in the fields or in the heart. Each day brings first light to bring life to the world. Where you find new life, there you will find first light as well."

I begin to understand. Something new has happened to me in this garden. My heart beats with new sounds, becomes one with the bird songs of this garden. My life has changed forever for having followed this trail of beauty. The first light of every day carries the first light of the first day as a promise. It's true—I have received new life. Yet I still do not know exactly how I got here. I followed the beautiful bird song in the near darkness of the dawn-to-be. I do not even know what trail I took. I simply followed.

"Beautiful Mother of Life," I dare to ask, "I don't even know how I got here. I think I know now what you're trying to teach me. But I know that once I leave you, I will never find this place again."

"Yes you will, Juanito, for it will find you."

"Dear Mother of the Living God, how can a path find the traveler? How can that which is sought find the seeker?"

"Dear Juanito, does not the lover find the beloved? Does not the bridegroom seek his bride day and night until he finds her? The first light of each day announces God's love and, so, each dawn becomes a seeking, a searching for his beloved. That is why I am here. I have come searching for you on his behalf. His path found you, beckoned you to follow into the garden where life and light meet."

"Oh Abuelita, your words inflame my heart so

because I know they are true. But, Señora, how can I be found?"

"Juanito, Juanito, look around you, and, especially, within you. God's love is a path for your heart and, if you follow, it will lead to a garden full of life and light. Your heart, dear Juanito Dieguito, is both the way and the garden. Look around you, *nietecito* (little grandson), this garden and your heart are one."

"Most Beautiful Lady, I am beside myself, my heart soars away from me—it is no longer mine. You have allowed light to enter into the darkness of my soul and helped me find this secret garden. I feel life, new life, inside me. The world seems young again. Grant me, Señora, to remain. This is my home and my garden. I know it now. From here I will cut flowers of devotion for you the first light of every day. From here I will sing a song for you, every mañanita, and bless the holy name of our God."

For Reflection

- Can you identify points in your life where your creative light or any interior light was obscured? Could you describe this feeling of loss as a death? Reflect deeply and try to describe the relationship between the loss of light and the presence of death. What might the opposite relationship look like?

- Put yourself in the place of Juan Diego. Where would you be going when you heard the bird song? What would be the first thing you might notice in this secret garden? Why?

- If all our secret gardens come from the same source, how do you explain our cultural differences? The variety of religions? Given what you have learned, what dialogue *might you carry as a believing Christian to someone from another faith?*

- *How do you trim your Christmas tree? What could it say about your secret garden? If you were to trim it differently this year, what would you change? Why?*

Closing Prayer

God, fill me with the dawn of a new life and bring me to the secret garden where you look for me. Mother of all the Living, teach me like Juan Diego how to follow my heart to your Son and the love of our God. Make my heart as simple and pure as that of your servant, Juan Diego. Make my heart clean white linen to drape over the altar of my life. Upon it I will place freshly cut blossoms of devotion from the garden of my soul. And there I will sing mañanitas, first light songs, in your honor at the dawn of every day.

Notes

[1] Genesis 3:24; 3:20.

[2] Genesis 1:1-5.

JEANETTE RODRIGUEZ

Day Four
Granting a Mother's Wish

Coming Together in the Spirit

The miracle of having a child comes with no
guarantees. Many are challenged with infertility,
pregnancy complications or babies born with health
problems. Even if we are gifted with healthy children, our
concerns are just beginning. We worry about everything
that could cause them injury, pain, suffering or sadness.
My husband and I have been blessed with two children.
While our love is powerful, it is not a repellent against
sorrow or mistakes.

I remember the concerns of my own mother and
father. They each focused on different goals for me. Like
most parents, my father wanted me to be an honorable
person, established and successful in the world. But my
mother just wanted me to be happy, to blossom. She
would say that a happy person is one who knows he or
she is in the embrace of God.

My mother died in 1980. It was hard to be separated
from the only person on whose lap I could rest my head.
But she left behind a sense of her presence. Even though
she is no longer with me physically, I feel her love and am
sustained by it. Her unconditional acceptance reflects
what can be only a glimpse of the love of God.

The thing I miss most about my mother is her *cariño*, her unique expressions of affection. Here are some of the things my mother wrote to me:

- *Mi querida y adorado hijita de mi alma.* Not Dear Jeanette, but My dear and adored daughter of my soul.

- *Mi querida y linda hijita de mi corazon.* My dear and beautiful daughter of my heart, *te quiero y no tienes idea como deseo tener te en mis brazos y no tan lejos.* I love you and you have no idea how much I desire to have you in my arms instead of so far away.

- *Janecita preciosa, me siento muy orgullosa de ti porque eres buenca, dulce, caritatira; siempre trabajando por los pobres y necesitados. Todo lo que haces Dios te premiará.* Precious Jeanette, I am very proud of you because you are good, sweet and charitable, always working for the needy and the poor. All the good you do, God will reward you.

Defining Our Thematic Context

Maybe because of her indigenous roots, my mother's way of speaking resembles the conversation between Our Lady of Guadalupe and Juan Diego. There are similarities in their tone, their use of diminutives, their intimate affection. Both are dialogues of great affection that exude a mother's presence and elicit a child's boundless joy.

Now that I, too, am a mother, I understand more deeply my mother's hopes and affection for me and the kindness and providence of Our Lady of Guadalupe. What is a mother's wish? First, that her children are whole, healthy, happy and nurtured in relationship with others. Second, that they know the love of God, to be sustained by it, to gain strength and direction from it, to know that no matter what happens to them in this world, they will always be loved. And third, that they are so rich in this love that it overflows from them, transforming everyone they meet, transforming the world for their children and generations to come.

Opening Prayer

Dear Mother, source of all that is good and loving, help me remember the touching expression of God's love that was incarnated in my mother and in all those who care for me, by remembering these words of Isaiah:

> Can a woman forget her nursing child,
> or show no compassion for the child of her womb?
> Even these may forget,
> yet I will not forget you.
> See, I have inscribed you on the palms of my hands;
> your walls are continually before me.[1]

Guadalupe, Maternal One, help me to be a revelation of God's love to my own children and to those whom I have an opportunity to parent.

RETREAT SESSION FOUR

Juan Diego has heard the music, the singing of the birds. Now he hears a woman's voice calling to him; he follows it to its source. Nothing troubles his heart, he fears nothing. He is extremely happy and content. He has reached the top of the ancient hill Tepeyac and is transfixed by what he sees.

A woman stands before him, resplendent with beauty and light. In her presence he falls to his knees. He listens to her voice, to her word, which is full of praise, very tender, full of generous respect and warm affection.

Guadalupe: "Juanito, Juan Dieguito, the smallest of my children, know and understand that I am the Mother of the most true God, the Giver of Life...the Lord of the Universe.

"I want very much, greatly do I desire, that my sacred little house be built here where I shall show Him, exalt Him by making Him manifest: I shall present Him to all people in all of my own love, in my compassionate gaze, in my help, in my aid: because I am truly your compassionate mother, yours and of all who live together in this land, and of all the races of those who love me, those who call to me, those who seek me, those who trust in me, there I shall listen to their weeping, to their sadness, so as to remedy, to cure all their pain, their misery, their sorrow."

She tells Juan to go to the Bishop and make known her desire. He obeys, but returns to her that evening with sadness.

Juan: "He (the Bishop) said to me: 'Some other time you will come, I shall listen more calmly, and then I will look closely at why you have come, your desire, your will.' I believe, having thought about how he answered me, that he thinks that the house you want them to build you here is only an invention of mine, or that it does not come from your lips; I beg you, my Lady, Queen, my dear Maiden, to entrust some nobleman, someone who is esteemed, who is known, respected, honored, with carrying out your kind wish...I am a man of the fields,...it is not my place to tread or to be there where you send me,...please relieve me of this duty: I shall only cause pain on your face, in your heart; I shall fall under your anger, cause you displeasure."

Guadalupe: "Listen, smallest of my children, be assured that those who serve me are not few in number, nor are the messengers I could send to carry my voice, my word, that my will be done; but it is very necessary that you, personally, should go, that it be through your intercession that my wish, my will be realized."

Juan: "My Lady, may I not cause your face or your heart to grieve; with all pleasure will I go to carry your voice, your word."

Guadalupe commands Juan to return for a sign he is to take to the Bishop. Juan, however, gets distracted. His uncle is ill and he must go for a priest. Guadalupe encounters him on the other side of the hill, the path that he has taken to avoid meeting her.

Juan: "My Young One, my Smallest Daughter, my dear Maiden, I hope you are well; how are you this morning? I hope your dear little body feels well, my Lady, my dear Maiden? I shall trouble your face, your heart: because I must tell you, that one of your servants, my uncle, is gravely ill.... And now I must hurry to your little house in Mexico, to call one of the loved ones of Our Lord to go to hear his confession."

Guadalupe: "Listen, and guard in your heart, my dearest son, that there is nothing for you to fear, nothing to afflict you; let neither your face nor your heart be worried; do not fear this or any other illness, or any other pain or affliction."

Juan Diego, at these loving words, the loving voice of the Queen of Heaven, was filled with consolation, and his heart was set to rest.

As soon as the Heavenly Queen has given her command he takes to the road, straight to Mexico, walking contentedly. His heart is calm, because everything will be all right.[2]

For Reflection

- *Remember a time in your life when you were able to "rest your head on someone's lap." Can you remember being warm, safe, protected? Are you welcoming and nurturing for those in sorrow or need? In what way are you a maternal or paternal presence for others?*

- *Have you ever tried to avoid doing what you know God wants of you? For what reasons?*

- *Are you willing to deliver the gospel even though you know you will not be heard or believed? Give examples of how you might do this.*

- *In what ways will you be present to others? To Our Lady of Guadalupe? To her Son? What wish of Guadalupe will you grant her during or after this retreat?*

Closing Prayer

Do listen,
do be assured of it in your heart,
my littlest one,
that nothing at all should alarm you,
should trouble you,
nor in any way disturb
your countenance, your heart.
And do not be afraid of this pestilence,
nor of any other pestilence
or any rasping hardship.

For am I not here,
I, your Mother?
Are you not in the cool of my shadow?
In the breeziness of my shade?

Is it not I that am
your source of contentment?

Are you not cradled in my mantle?
cuddled in the crossing of my arms?

Is there anything else for you to need?[3]

Notes

[1] Isaiah 49:15-16.

[2] Nican mopohua. English translation by John Dierchsmeier, based on the Spanish translation by P. Mario Rojas.

[3] "Our Lady of Guadalupe to Juan Diego," CARA Studies on Popular Devotion, Volume 2: *Guadalupan Studies*, Monograph No. 6.

ANITA DE LUNA, M.C.D.P.

DAY FIVE

Accepting the Call to New Life

Coming Together in the Spirit

In Albuquerque, New Mexico, in August 1991, at their annual National Assembly, the Leadership Conference of Women Religious, representing the religious women of the United States, elected a new president.

On the day of election in the Fairmont Hotel ballroom, three candidates sat on an elevated platform. I was one of them. We were each introduced and called to accept our nominations in a short speech. Being from a small southern community, I felt inadequate and unsure about my nomination. I was overwhelmed by the size of the room, and terrified at the prospect of speaking in front of the illustrious leaders assembled there. As I stepped up to the microphone, I saw an image of Our Lady of Guadalupe draped across the back of the stage.

A quick glance at the image gave me the courage I needed. "*Virgen Santa*," I prayed. "If this address to this conference for this five minutes is all you are asking me to do, I must do this moment justice."

Standing before the conference, I addressed the nine hundred religious leaders gathered there. Present in my mind were the words of my mother, "*Si puedes ayudarles, hijita y si te lo piden, hazlo.*" (If you can help them, my little daughter, and if they are asking your help, do it.)

The following day from the same podium the results were announced: "The conference has elected a new president. We extend our congratulations, and we pledge our support and prayers to Sister Anita de Luna."

This was a big calling, one demanding self-denial and a willingness to be stretched beyond my present limits. As it had the day I made my first vows, the idea of discipleship crystallized for me. I was leaving the familiar and moving toward the unknown. I had to set aside my personal agendas, my small community's concerns, and serve the needs of the U.S. religious throughout the conference. From that call to serve the universal Church, many reflections were born. That yes, that *si*, would change me, transforming my life. I struggled giving birth to that *fiat*. I resisted accepting the reality of what that election meant. I cried in my vulnerability and asked "why me?" I prayed for strength and courage, for ability and wisdom, and felt ill-prepared for the task.

As I considered the role, God was with me and la Morenita inspired me and kept me close to her. At certain moments I felt confident; many times I was sure someone else could do the job better. I captured my initial response in verse that August day; it still inspires my spirit and stretches my comfort zone. I wrote:

> Your call has shaken me like the gust of a stormy
> wind.
> From where shall come the answers to the questions
> yet to be?
> This task, like shoes a size too big, is hard to fill.
> I still wear the threads of my barrio dress.
> And now I am called to global attire.

I wrestle with unfamiliarity and foreignness surrounds
  me.
I am made to let go of what comfortably fits. I feel
  exposed, not fitting in this new robe.
Protect my vulnerability with your mantle, Virgen
  Morena.
Under your shadow may I be made secure.

Defining Our Thematic Context

At my election, I felt very much like Juan Diego in his
insecurity as well as in his trust and reliance on the Virgin.
The task the Virgin gives Juan Diego is that of being a
disciple of courage and an ambassador of reconciliation.
The call to discipleship always has a personal price tag
that one must be willing to pay. We read in the Gospel:

> If any want to become my followers, let them deny
> themselves and take up their cross and follow me.[1]

In the Old Testament the covenant makers Abraham,
Moses and David entered into a relationship with Yahweh
and received a promise of God's presence and protection.
So also in the New Testament, along with the cost of
discipleship there is the promise of divine presence. After
Jesus leaves his disciples, he promises the Spirit will
remain among them. We are not left alone; graces,
commensurate with our tasks, are made accessible to us.
The mandate is: Be transformed.

Discipleship in some ways is like a new birth. We are
called to announce the Good News in a way peculiarly
our own and to image or bring forth a new creation. It
calls for donning a new robe as in Paul's "new creation."
"So if anyone is in Christ, there is a new creation:
everything old has passed away: see, everything has

become new!"[2] The call to which we respond is one of becoming instruments of God for the message. "So we are ambassadors for Christ, since God is making his appeal through us."[3]

So it is with Juan Diego who is commissioned by the Mother of God to participate in bringing about a new creation, a new identity for himself and to his people. As Juan Diego becomes a new person, confident of his mission, so also the indigenous nation is reborn of a new Mother with tenderness, compassion and infinite care.

Each day we wake up we are invited to participate in bringing forth new life, by adding joy to the day, by supporting family and friends who need it, by being present to those who are lonely or simply by greeting and giving a smile to a passerby. All are invitations to counter some of the death and negativity that clouds the creative energy given us by God. We are invited daily to give life, to give birth, to recreate a moment and make our small part of the world a bit more pleasant, more aware of God's love, more reflective of the goodness that is inside of us. Like Juan Diego, we must listen closely to hear and be receptive to how we are being invited to participate in God's plan.

Opening Prayer

Lady of Guadalupe, we come before you to ask that
  you hear our prayer.
Help us to be life-givers by proclaiming your message
  of salvation to all people.
Fill our hearts with your compassion and your love.
Give hope to those who suffer because of ignorance,
  poverty and injustice.
Kind and gracious Mother, just as one day in Tepeyac,

you recreated an oppressed culture with beauty and
with dignity; grant us the grace to engender
consolation for your people in these days of
alienation and division.

Just as you encouraged Juan Diego to be your
collaborator and ambassador in a new creation, a
new alternative, grant us the grace to be agents of
reconciliation and proclaimers of the Good News of
your Son.

Bless us with courage to serve, creativity to open new
vistas and generosity and enthusiasm in
contributing to the faith lives of those with whom
we live or to whom we are sent.

Give us a desire to be transformed followers of your
Son and help us give birth to a more just and
reconciled family and society.

We ask for your intercession in our prayer and for
your enduring tenderness and protection in our
days of service among our families, in our
neighborhoods, our churches and our world.

Amen.

RETREAT SESSION FIVE

Juan Diego has gone to the palace of the bishop to
deliver the Lady's message and met with rejection. He
feels his poverty, his insecurity and his inadequacy. He
blames himself for the bishop's inattentiveness. He is not
credible before this official of the Church. How many
times have we experienced rejection from persons in
authority and power, sometimes from our family members
and friends? The feeling makes us want to quit and not try

again. Yet even Jesus, the Son of God, spoke about expecting to be rejected. He said: "...the Son of Man must undergo great suffering, and be rejected by the elders, the chief priests, and the scribes...."[4]

In the bishop's house, Juan Diego sees his faded poncho and his worn sandals and feels foreign in this elegant place. He takes in the scent of the waxed floors and fresh coffee as he waits. He hears the hushed voices denying him entrance into the bishop's quarters, before they are addressed to him directly. He grows self-conscious of the dust on his sandals and the dirt on his pants, and he is keenly aware of how they contrast with the clean brown habits of the Franciscan friars who pass back and forth before him.

After much insistence, Juan Diego is finally allowed into the bishop's quarters. He is received but senses the bishop's disbelief. His heart is heavy as he walks slowly back to the Lady to deliver the message that he has failed in his mission. He thinks of how she entrusted her desire to him and feels beaten for not being able to help her. He wishes he had a more commanding presence that would have made the bishop listen. He wishes he had words that would be impressive and could have spoken more convincingly of the things the lovely Lady wanted. If only he were different, then maybe they would have listened. If he had been wearing different clothes, perhaps if his skin was a different color he would have made a better impression with the bishop.

> In dejection, he approaches Tepeyac and says to the Virgin: "My Keeper, my Patroness, my Lady, the least of my daughters, My Little One, I went where you sent me to take your thoughts, your word. With great difficulty I entered the place of the bishop, I saw him, before him I spoke your thoughts and your word, just as you asked. He received me well enough

and listened attentively. But according to how he responded to me; I do not think his heart was receptive, he did not believe me. He said: 'You must return again, I will listen more calmly, I still must see, I will contemplate well from its beginning this for which you have come, your will and your desire.' I saw perfectly, from the way in which he responded, that he thinks that maybe I am inventing that you wish a temple built, and that maybe that is not your wish."[5]

Sometimes the things we must do are difficult. At times the people to whom we are sent are not receptive to us. Those close to us turn a deaf ear to what we say and those who do not know us do not listen. Often there are feelings of vulnerability and uncertainty in what we do, even when we feel we are doing a good thing and we want to complete a task. Frequently we feel like Juan Diego, that someone else would do so much better than we. Like him, we look at ourselves and find we fall short as much as we try to compensate for what we lack. We think others have more or know more than we do or can do something so much easier than we can. It is in those times that we must remember that our weakness can be a strength. We remember Saint Paul's words:

Consider your own call, brothers and sisters: not many of you were wise by human standards, not many were powerful, not many were of noble birth. But God chose what is foolish in the world to shame the wise; God chose what is weak in the world to shame the strong; God chose what is low and despised in the world, things that are not, to reduce to nothing things that are....[6]

Juan Diego continues his conversation with the Virgin, trying to explain his unworthiness to act as her ambassador because of his frailty and his lack of a polished personality. He says:

> That is why, I implore you, My Keeper, my Queen,
> my little daughter, to send one of your worthy noble
> ones, the known, appreciated and respectable ones,
> to them you entrust the deliverance of your word,
> your message, so that it may be believed. Because,
> surely, I am a laborer from nowhere, a small ladder,
> the dung of the city, I am a leaf, a no one that has to
> be carried: and you, my daughter, the least, my Little
> One, My Lady, my Queen, you send me to a place
> amidst where I do not pass or stop.[7]

Juan Diego speaks in clear recognition that he is limited in
who he is and how he is seen by society. He and his
people are perceived as an unworthy, conquered race. The
total weight of his defeat comes upon him. He is
overwhelmed by the importance of the task the Virgin
desires. How often do we feel like Juan Diego? We
recognize our limitations and the tasks before us seem so
immense compared to what we can do. These feelings are
very common. In fact, Jesus makes these feelings of
inadequacy part of the condition for discipleship. In his
second prediction of his death and resurrection he speaks
to his disciples saying:

> "Whoever wants to be first must be last of all and
> servant of all." Then he took a little child and put it
> among them; and taking it in his arms, he said to
> them, "Whoever welcomes one such child in my
> name welcomes me, and whoever welcomes me
> welcomes not me but the one who sent me."[8]

In the time of Jesus, children were not important, not
worthy of attention, so to be a child was to be
marginalized, to be insignificant. This teaching follows the
disciples' argument about who was the greatest among
them. Jesus' answer explains that our vulnerability and

lack of confidence allow God to help us. They are God's way of saying to us, "I am here to carry my part, you need not feel you must have all that is required. We are partners in this task." So the Mother of God is not dissuaded by Juan Diego's feelings of defeat and futility. She still wishes him to be her messenger and responds to his litany of defeat:

> "Listen, the least of my children, know in your heart...I very much implore you, the least of my children, and with all energy I ask that it be precisely tomorrow that you return again to see the bishop. And let him know for me, have him hear well my will and desire so that he may erect my temple. Tell him once more that I, the ever Virgin Mary, Mother of God, Teotl, send you."⁹

The Mother of God acknowledges his fears but still, she chooses him. The Virgin dresses Juan Diego with a new garment of affirmation; she gives him renewed confidence by re-identifying him with her trust and her election of him. His self-worth is lifted because someone who is very significant believes in him and entrusts to him a role of collaboration in a very important project.

What a difference we make when we affirm others. When we believe in them, we help them believe in themselves. Sometimes our first effort will not be successful, but someone will help us try again. The self-confidence we gain from succeeding makes us look at ourselves in a new way. We are able to do things we could not do before. La Morenita brought to life to Juan Diego as a confident disciple. But she also brought new life to an entire nation, as she was recognized in her mestiza presence as the Mother of God. She brought a new dignity to a people who were dying in collective defeat.

The Lady looked tenderly at Juan Diego as she spoke

her assurances. She reached toward him to bless him and leaned over to place her hands over him and her mantle brushed against him as she drew near. For a moment, he was transfixed with her beauty and her tenderness. He felt all insecurity leave him and he received the grace of courage. He was aware of the warmth of her hands as she touched his head. She had assured him that she would support him and be with him.

> My Keeper, my Lady, My Little One, do not let me put worry on your face, in your heart. With all the good will in my heart, I will go, I will go there to speak in truth, your thought and your word. In no way will I keep from doing so, nor will the journey be hard. I will go to do your will. It could be that I will not be heard and if I am heard, perhaps I will not be believed. Tomorrow in the evening when the sun goes down, I will return with the response from the bishop.[10]

Juan Diego accepts his recommissioning and is filled with realistic hope as he bids farewell to the Virgin. He believes that she has the power to make things possible and is strengthened in his participation with the divine plan. How unfortunate we are when we are not receptive to the grace of God. How unfortunate if Juan Diego would not have listened to the Mother of God. His destiny and that of an entire nation would have been very different. We are reminded of the rich young man from the Gospel of Mark who asks what must he do to be a follower and Jesus responds: "...go, sell what you own, and give the money to the poor...then come, follow me."[11] Scripture tells us that the young man walked away sadly because he could not part with his riches and thus could not participate in God's plan. He would not allow himself to be transformed, to be born again.

Juan Diego's lightheartedness and light-footedness in returning to his task speak of his trust and love for the Mother of God. It underscores his renewed confidence and recommitment. Faith and receptivity to conversion and new life are essential to discipleship. The rich young man's account is a sharp contrast to the many characters in the Gospels, who like Juan Diego, are amenable to God's call to be reborn. One such character is the blind Bartimaeus at Jericho. We read:

> When he heard that it was Jesus of Nazareth, he began to shout out and say, "Jesus, Son of David, have mercy on me!"...Jesus stood still and said, "Call him here." And they called the blind man, saying to him, "Take heart; get up, he is calling you." So throwing off his cloak, he sprang up and came to Jesus. Then Jesus said to him, "What do you want me to do for you?" The blind man said to him, "My teacher, let me see again." Jesus said to him, "Go, your faith has made you well." Immediately he regained his sight and followed him on the way.[12]

Seeing as we have not seen before is part of the experience of conversion, it is part of a new life we receive when we renounce the familiar. We experience the joy displayed by Juan Diego and the sighted Bartimaeus as opposed to the heaviness of the rich young man who walks away sadly. Shedding the weight of the old life, we see Bartimaeus throw off his old cloak and Juan Diego dressed in a new identity for himself and his people. The signs of their new life are energy, joy and consolation, and it is these same signs that manifest harmony with God and with each other in our lives.

For Reflection

- *Insecure and self-conscious, Juan Diego accepts a mission to visit the bishop with a message on behalf of the Lady of Guadalupe. What are the unexplored territories to which you are being called? Are feelings of insecurity and inadequacy keeping you from responding to the call to collaborate in new projects that could mean more abundant life for you or someone else? What will you do about these feelings?*

- *Juan Diego rightly perceived the bishop's rejection of him and felt he had failed. He begged the Lady to send someone else. When have you experienced real or imagined rejection? The Lady of Guadalupe recommissioned Juan Diego. Who will help you try again when you feel you have failed?*

- *Juan Diego's collaboration with the Lady brought a nation that felt ashamed of its birthright to claim a noble mother and regain its dignity and cultural beauty. Which opportunities do you have now to contribute beauty and new birth in your life or in the life of someone else? How will you fulfill these opportunities?*

Closing Prayer

Litany to Our Lady of Guadalupe

Mother of the unborn,   *pray for us*
Mother of orphans,
Mother of the rejected,
Mother of the unwanted,
Mother of the unrecognized,
Mother of the powerless,
Mother of the voiceless,

Mother of the oppressed,
Mother of migrants,
Mother of the marginalized,
Mother of the destitute,
Mother of foreigners,
Mother of immigrants,
Mother of the homeless,
Mother of those considered giftless,
Mother of the those who see no value in their lives,
Mother of those who have no political influence,
Mother of those who have no reason to hope.

From becoming oppressive,   *deliver us*
From becoming cynical,
From denying options to the poor,
From becoming opportunists,
From becoming deaf to the voices of prophets,
From becoming blind to injustice,
From becoming complacent,
From becoming ungrateful servants,
From becoming arrogant,
From becoming elitists.

Model of love and compassion,   *may we imitate you*
Model of hope and new life,
Model of evangelization,
Model of simplicity,
Model of justice for the poor,
Enabler of the downtrodden,
Example of receptivity,
Example of humility,
Example of sensitivity,
Bridge builder of cultures,
Respecter of diversity,
Mother of consolation,

Mother of those who say "yes" to Jesus
Mother of Providence.[13]

Let us pray:

Virgen Morena, "Dark Virgin," Mother of God, Lady of Guadalupe, we commit ourselves to follow your example, to be life-givers and be receptive to new life. We will be faithful followers in your love toward the poor, in your desire to give dignity to all people and to treat all the abandoned with tenderness. Let us live with constant confidence that we need not fear when we acknowledge you as our Mother, Mother of God. Grant that we may participate in your plan for new life and give us faith in the daily miracles that you and your Son, Jesus, work in our lives. Amen.

Notes

[1] Mark 8:34.

[2] 2 Corinthians 5:17.

[3] 2 Corinthians 5:20.

[4] Mark 8:31.

[5] Acuna, Clodomiro L. Siller, *El Mensaie de Maria de Guadalupe* (Buenos Aires: Editorial Guadalupe, 1989), p. 29.

[6] 1 Corinthians 1:26-28.

[7] Acuna, p. 29.

[8] Mark 9:35-37.

[9] Acuna, p. 31.

[10] Acuna, p. 31.

[11] Mark 10:21.

[12] Mark 10:47-52.

[13] Luna, Anita de, *MCDP Post Autonomy Reflections* (San Antonio: MCDP Publications, 1994), p. 74.

ROSENDO URRABAZO, C.M.F.

DAY SIX

Seeking Life's Miracles

*Meditation on the Healing of Bernadino
in the Story of Our Lady of Guadalupe*

Coming Together in the Spirit

Many years past I saw a young child in a hospital
burn unit that I will forever remember. He was about three
years old and had been in the family garage playing.
Somehow he found some matches and in his curiosity
began playing with them, not knowing that nearby was a
container full of gasoline. There was an explosion and
eighty percent of his small body was severely burned. He
had no face, no fingers or toes. His eyes, ears, nose were
gone. His body was ashen black. Were it not for the
morphine they gave him, he would have been in
tremendous pain. Mercifully, he was unconscious, but at
first his heartbeat was strong. There was nothing that
could be done for him. It was only a matter of time.

I visited as part of my normal rounds as a hospital
chaplain. I met his parents. They were a young couple
with only a painful sadness on their faces. They said
nothing to me. They only stared at their child and held
each other. There was no need for words. Their faces and

the baby's body said it all.

I was shocked by such a horrible sight. I struggled to find words of consolation for that couple. I could not even find any for myself. How could this happen? Where was God? His guardian angel? His parents? Who had been watching out for this child? I kept these questions to myself. I stayed with this family for a long time. We never spoke a word. I hoped that my presence was somehow a sign of my concern and what we call in Spanish *acompanamento* (accompaniment). Later that day the baby died. I never saw the parents again. I will never forget the look on their faces as they watched their baby slowly die.

Defining Our Thematic Context

Like the biblical Job, I ask, "Why did this happen?" It is wonderful to hear stories of miraculous healing, but more often than not there is no healing, only suffering and death. Why are some healed and others not? Is it a question of faith? Perhaps in some cases it is just tragedy, and there is no answer, and the only purpose it has is the one we choose to give it.

This is a difficult reflection. It is about one healing. But it is also about the suffering of many who cry out to God.

What role do miracles play in life? On this sixth day of our retreat we meditate upon the miraculous healing of Juan Diego's uncle Bernadino. Miraculous healing has been a part of the Christian religious tradition since the time of Christ. In Scripture, Jesus constantly reminds us that it is the faith of the sufferer (or friends, or family) that has brought about the healing.[1] In our own time, prayer meetings give praise to God for the healings that take place during their services. Healings are a part of the Christian message. Still there remain many unanswered questions about these healings and about the purpose of illness and death. Is sickness a punishment from God? Or is it just part of being alive? Is death a part of our fall from God's grace? What about the innocent who suffer from illness, starvation and incurable disease? Is there a purpose for their pain?

Opening Prayer

Dear God, be patient with my questions and doubts. Know that I seek to do your will. There is so much I do not understand. There are so many unanswered questions. Help me be at peace with my doubts and act in ways that bring healing to others. I pray for my own healing and for the spiritual and physical healing of your people. I believe that you want us all to be healthy and that illness and death are not part of your gracious love for us. Because of this you have sent us your Son Jesus to heal us and to remind us that death is not the end but only a new beginning of life in your love. Help me to fight against suffering and death in all its forms that your Kingdom might begin here in the present; let your will for our well-being be our constant comfort.

RETREAT SESSION SIX

In the middle of his experiences at Tepeyac, Juan Diego's attention is suddenly focused on his uncle Bernadino. Gravely ill, Bernadino relies on Juan to bring a priest to hear his confession and prepare him for death. Dutifully, Juan takes a new route to the city on that day, one that will take him around the other side of the hill of Tepeyac. Time is precious and he knows he cannot afford to be stopped by another apparition. But Our Lady of Guadalupe comes to him anyway, finds out his concern and tells him not to trouble himself about the errand any more: His uncle will recover. She then sends him again on her own errand. Unknown to Juan at that time, she also appears to his uncle Bernadino and heals him. It is a miracle.

Juan Diego set out to fulfill his family duty, even though he thought it would deprive him of an unimaginable personal joy—a visit with the Mother of God. He makes this sacrifice without complaint or sorrow; he even goes out of his way to avoid the pleasure that would delay him. Many of us might have criticized his decision, thinking that he should fulfill his higher obligations first. But Juan responded to the one who needed him most and, it seems, Our Lady approved of his decision.

Is it an illusion to believe that we are responsible for the well-being and happiness of others? We cannot make decisions for others; we cannot live their lives. We can only love and support, encourage and perhaps give some assistance. There is much that happens that we cannot control. Still there is something inside us that when confronted with pain and suffering wants to do everything possible to get rid of it. Many times though, as with the child in the burn unit, there is absolutely nothing we can do. We just feel helpless.

Juan Diego must have wondered why his uncle was so afflicted that he now lay dying. What did he do to deserve such suffering? I have thought, at times, that God is cruel to give us life only to take it away. The Bible offers a number of explanations for suffering and death. At times, sickness is seen as a punishment for wrongdoing.

Consider the plagues of Egypt and how the Egyptians were punished for their disbelief in the God of Moses and the Hebrew people.[2] In another passage illness is not punishment from God but a test of faith. In the story of Job, God allows the devil to bring havoc upon him and his family to test his fidelity to God.[3] Sickness, death and misfortune in this story come from the devil but with God's permission. Job's friends challenge him to examine his life and figure out what he did to deserve such misfortune. Job is steadfast in his belief that he has done nothing wrong and cries out to God for justice.[4] He dares to ask "Why?" His question is answered only with his own silence and awe at the majesty of a God who owes him no explanation.[5]

Jesus answers the same question in reference to the man born blind.[6] "Who sinned..." he is asked, "this man or his parents?" What does it mean when Jesus says, "...he was born blind so that God's works might be revealed in him"?[7] Is he talking about the illness or the cure? He goes on to accuse the Pharisees of spiritual blindness. They claim to understand (to see) God's law, yet are blind to the person and good works of Jesus. Throughout his public life, Jesus healed that God might be glorified. God is not glorified in sickness, but in the cure.

It is not God's will that we should suffer. Consider how much of Jesus' ministry is spent healing people and teaching them how to live fuller lives. Guadalupe heals Bernadino, giving him new life. And he is but the first to receive the gift she brings. She calls all of us in the Americas to new life as one people in the Lord. In her, an oppressed and defeated people found hope and dignity. Where there was death she brought life. Where there was humiliation she brought respect. Her image radiates both power and tenderness. She overshadows the past and brings her people into a new future, a new beginning. She reminds us that God has not forgotten us.

But we have forgotten each other. Finding work, food, clothes, drink, housing, medicine are all daily chores that challenge the human spirit and bring us into contact with one another. But for many, it is an impossible challenge. Most people in the world barely survive each day. A few enjoy the world's riches while most suffer privation. Those who have nothing cry out in their need and desperation. They find themselves oppressed by the political will of others and the chaos of conflicting national and international financial interests.

They look to the first world, to us, for salvation, not understanding that the price of our security is often our souls. To be secure is to be blind to the needs of others. To be safe is to be deaf to the pain of others. To eat well is to starve others. Who is there to face the demons around us? Who will name the evil that consumes our world? Juan Diego did what one man can do. He cared about one other person. He left aside other tasks, important as they were, divinely inspired though they may have been, and lovingly went about helping one other person. Still, Guadalupe called him to be more. She calls us to do more, to be more for others. Her message of hope for the people of the Americas is more than charitable concern for others. Her presence questions the very structure of our society and its many ills. Why are people hungry? Why are people naked, thirsty, in need of work, housing and medicine? I see in her call to Juan Diego a challenge for all of us to step outside ourselves and call the world of oppression to task. She calls on the world to be one community of men and women who see each other as brothers and sisters. The miracle of Bernadino's healing is one step toward the healing of the world's pain.

And the miracle is not only that of Bernadino but the salvation (the coming to wholeness) of Juan Diego as well.

He had within him the seed of God's love which he demonstrated in his concern for others. Guadalupe takes that basic goodness that God offers to each of us and helps Juan Diego to accept his call to speak for her and for his people. He hesitates, stumbles, falls flat on his face in failure and returns to her discouraged and disappointed. He sees himself as an unworthy representative and begs her to choose someone else. But Guadalupe is relentless in her patience and determination that he will be her ambassador. She chooses him. He must learn to believe in her choice, to let go of his own self-judgment and poor self-concept. Mary understands. She was also afraid and confused when God first called her into his service.[8]

We, too, are called into God's service. Still, we are only too well aware of our own failings and shortcomings. Maybe we feel that God should choose someone else, but we continue to hear in moments of deep silence, "I choose you." We are only asked to do what we can. Juan Diego could not heal his uncle, but he could bring him the comfort of his faith; in doing this, he became the instrument of a true miracle.

Guadalupe's call to us is to do the same as Juan Diego: Build a temple. Today in the Americas we don't need more buildings, but we do need to build up the faith of our people in God and in themselves. We are called to proclaim the love of God and to show that love in a life of service for others. In addition to the responsibilities we have for ourselves, our families, our jobs and our friends, we are also responsible for others in this world. We may not be to blame for the many problems of our world, but we are responsible to help find solutions. We must choose to believe in the goodness within us and in others. We must see ourselves as God sees us—all people are God's and deserve to be treated with respect and dignity. The healing Guadalupe brings is not the conversion of natives to a particular denomination or religion but to a respect for life that gives praise and glory to the Creator of life—a way of life that has been made known to us by great prophets and teachers in all the major religious traditions of the world and in a special way in the person of Jesus of Nazareth whom we Christians call the Christ.

All people, all religions, all cultures—believers and non-believers—are invited to know the message of God's son and servant, Jesus. He calls on all to believe in God's bountiful and merciful love for each of us. This is much bigger than any ideology or any one religion. Our religious institutions are called to help us in developing our relationship with God and with each other. They accompany us, challenge us and guide us along our journey.

The name of Guadalupe means "the one who crushes the head of the serpent." There is evil in the world. It waits for our tiredness and inattention, our neediness, our loneliness. We cannot expect God to crush the evil within us, within our world. To take away the shadow is to take away that which creates the shadow. But we can ask for the power to recognize evil as evil. We can hope to understand our own limitations and those of others and make up for them with the overflowing love of God.

It is not for heaven that we should live righteous lives. It is not for the eternal rewards that have been imagined and hoped for since the promises of Christ. Even if there were no heaven, if there were no hell or purgatory or eternal judgment, we must still seek to live lives worthy of the gift of life itself.

Guadalupe, there is so much pain and suffering in the world. What can I do? What path should I take? Guide me as you did Juan Diego to dream bigger dreams, to help others and to challenge those structures and institutions that keep people poor and hungry and homeless. There is an indifference that can be so subtle and so acceptable among us who live in a land of plenty. There is what seems to be a kind of institutionalized tolerance of evil that pervades our social structures. It is an acceptable tolerance of the suffering of others as inevitable and even at times necessary. It is at times cloaked in nationalism, but more often is blatant disregard for anyone who is poor or different.

Let me not be deceived by evil. Let me not embrace the seduction to wealth and position as grace. Rather anything I have or have inherited let me put at the service of others. Let me walk in God's justice. Let me, like Juan Diego, listen to your gentle call to build up God's kingdom and not my own. Walk alongside me as you guided the steps of Juan Diego and create in me the miracle of my own conversion. Be a mantle that covers me, a shield that protects me.

Teach me what you taught Juan Diego. You lovingly called him Juan Dieguito, little Diego. He lovingly spoke to you in his native language at once with familiarity and with respect. Madre, you who speak the language of the heart, you who speak to us in the symbols of your image, speak to me about my own death and what awaits me after this life. I know that until I can come to terms with my own death I will only strive to preserve my own life and my own will. Teach me to let go of my will, to lose my life that I might freely give of myself to others in the work of justice.

Now, even more than before, we have reason to bless God our Creator, for one like us has shown us the way. Thanks to you we have the example and the Word that is Jesus. Mary, you brought his message to the new world and now there are millions who believe because of you. It was you and your missionaries that made these miracles of faith possible.

Make it so in my life also, that I can add to the list of those who celebrate your "yes" to God and the gift of your Son. Help me see the miracle that is life and when my moment of existence is ended, whether suddenly or after many years, help me to let go and, like the leaves carried by the autumn winds, let me go dancing.

For Reflection

- *Read Job 1. What do you think of his response to personal tragedy? Where does that kind of faith come from? What would your reaction be? How have you responded to tragedy in the past? What has been your experience with regard to miraculous healing?*

- *Is there a tension in your life between obligation to family and a call to service? What do you think of Juan Diego's choice? What has been your decision in the past?*

- *What still needs healing in your life? What kind of healing is needed in our society? What steps can you take to bring this healing about?*

- *Read Exodus 6-12. Meditate upon the plagues of Egypt. What are the plagues of today? Do they originate from God? How do people bring upon themselves "plagues"? To what extent are these natural events that we give supernatural purpose? Does it help to say that they come from God or from the devil?*

- *Should we try to give meaning to the suffering of the innocent? Is there a Christian way of understanding pain and death? What is your response?*

- *What miracle do you most desire for the world today? How will you petition and collaborate with Our Lady of*

Guadalupe and her Son, Jesus, to help make this miracle happen?

Closing Prayer

Lord, Guadalupe's healing of Bernadino, Jesus' teachings and miracles, and all of your creation sing the inestimable value of life. With gratitude for all your gifts, we ask that you show us the sanctity of all life and teach us to preserve it. Give us the courage to risk insecurity to help those in danger, to speak to help those without a voice, to sacrifice a sumptuous meal to help the starving. We know too well that there is evil in the world beyond our control. Give us the wisdom to recognize and challenge the evil we can control.

Help us to understand how our selfish actions create the suffering of others and give us the grace to be become selfless, a gate through which your love can flow, healing the world. Amen.

Notes

1 Matthew 17:14-22, Mark 7:24-30, Luke 8:40-56.
2 Exodus 6:14-12:30.
3 Job 1:8-11.
4 Job 6:24.
5 Job 40:3-5.
6 John 9:1-41.
7 John 9:3.
8 Luke 1:29-30.

VIRGILIO ELIZONDO

Day Seven
Recognizing a Mother's Presence

Coming Together in the Spirit

From his heavenly home, Blessed Juan Diego
contemplates the events of 1531—unnoticed and certainly
not recorded by historians but engraved deeply in the
hearts and memories of the people. I imagine how he
might speak to us:

> The four days since she first appeared to me on
> Mount Tepeyac were incredible. So many things
> happened so fast—the most beautiful and the ugliest,
> the most uplifting and the most humiliating, the
> most life-giving and the most devastating. Thank
> you for staying on the journey with me. Quite often,
> I was quite discouraged, but the vivid memory of
> her presence and her tender and compassionate
> words gave me the courage to continue. After all, she
> had assured me: "You have nothing to fear. Am I not
> here, who is your compassionate mother?"
>
> I was totally startled when she suddenly appeared
> on my tilma (shoulder cape). As if painted by divine
> hands, she suddenly appeared. She was just as
> beautiful as when I had first seen her and full of the
> look of love and compassion. Her eyes reflected all of

us who were gazing at her. There she was for all to see just as I had seen her.

I never dreamed she would stay with us and with all generations to come. She really meant far more than I could have ever comprehended at that moment when she said to me that she wanted to be present to all her children, all the inhabitants of these lands.

All of a sudden, she wasn't only mine, she was everyone's. Her words kept ringing in every fiber of my being: "I am the mother of all the inhabitants of this land." In my wildest dreams, I could never have imagined the full meaning of her presence throughout the Americas and throughout the centuries. I could never even begin to count the millions of miracles which have been brought about through her intercession. She continues to make a difference in more and more people every day. At first, she was present only to me, then to the bishop and his attendants, but now, her presence has no limits.

Defining Our Thematic Context

As a priest, I can begin to appreciate Blessed Juan Diego's wonder at the providential events of 1531. Having been ordained thirty-three years, I sometimes look back on that precious moment immediately before my priestly ordination. As I laid facedown, prostrated before the main altar of the church where I had been baptized, in San Antonio, and as the choir and congregation sang the litany of the saints, thousands of thoughts rushed through my mind. It was as if I was reliving my whole life in a few brief instants. I was both excited and scared. I was much more aware of my deficiencies and weaknesses than of my talents and strengths. I certainly did not feel worthy. Yet, when asked, the people who had known me all my life confirmed that they wanted me to be their priest. I couldn't wait for the litany to end so that the Archbishop would impose hands on me. Still, as it came closer to that time, I became all the more fearful.

In those precious moments of being totally alone with my God, in spite of the fact that I was surrounded by a church packed with friends and supporters, I was tempted to run away. Yet I regained my strength when in my thoughts I heard the same voice and words which blessed Juan Diego heard: "You have nothing to fear. Am I not here who am your mother?"

As I look back, I can say honestly say that, with the grace of God, I have been able to accomplish many exciting and life-giving works, from helping sinners rejoice in the mercy of God, to helping the dying into the joys of eternal life, to walking the streets in the ritual celebrations of the people, and many other fruitful ministries—far beyond anything I could ever have imagined possible. I never dreamed the priesthood could be so rewarding and far-reaching. I am still very much aware of my weakness and deficiencies, but I am constantly grateful and rejoice in the wonders God continues to work through me. I can truthfully say with Mary of Nazareth: "My whole being rejoices in God my savior who has done great things for me."

Opening Prayer

O Blessed Juan Diego, walk with me and share with me your ability to accept with confidence, excitement and joy the unexpected interventions of God in my life and in the lives of my family and friends. Help me to understand that I do not have to know exactly how things will work out. Help me to overcome my fears of inadequacy and the pains of rejection. Help me to be patient, especially when God places detours and delays in my intended ways. Let your confidence and courage become my own as I continue on the pilgrimage of life.

RETREAT SESSION SEVEN

Isn't it amazing how one quiet event can change the world? Jesus was born and resurrected in the middle of night, in the midst of the poor; Our Lady of Guadalupe appeared to an unknown Indian on the outskirts of Mexico City. Neither event was widely chronicled by contemporary historians. Yet these two events have transformed the world—more than even the victories of the Roman Empire, the coronation of kings and queens, or the victories of the recent world wars.

Unnoticed by the powers of the world, or even our closest friends, God continues to enter into our lives. Quietly but powerfully, God intervenes for our salvation. The Guadalupe story, like the story of Jesus of Nazareth, is a marvelous manifestation of the way in which God enters into our lives: subtly, quietly, unseen.

Devotion to Our Lady of Guadalupe continues to grow throughout the Americas. The official Church has more tolerated it than promoted it, and the liturgy has difficulty celebrating it during the season of Advent—as if God had made a mistake in allowing the apparitions to take place at that time. Yet there is no feast that is celebrated with such an increasing fervor by the faithful than that of Our Lady of Guadalupe on December 12.

And it is not just the celebration on the feast day. Artists continue to depict her, public murals place her in a position of honor, parishes and schools reenact the basic story every year, television shows constantly refer to her, girls and boys are named after her, home shrines continue to be built.

I will never forget a day shortly before the American forces were to be sent to the Persian Gulf. A young man and a young woman who were in the military came to me. They wanted me to bless their tattoos of Our Lady of Guadalupe. At first I was taken aback, as I had never before received such a request. So I asked them if a medal wouldn't have been a better idea. And the young man said, "But, Father, we might have lost a medal. And we didn't want to lose her. We wanted her to stay with us. So that's why we had her tattooed close to our hearts."

That was such a profound moment for me. Nobody had told that young couple to do that. They simply intuited that this was a way to keep Guadalupe close to their hearts. No order of priests or religious was promoting tattoos, after all.

Historians question Our Lady of Guadalupe's authenticity while the faithful question the authenticity of the historians who question her. Liturgists put her down only to be ignored by the faithful, the clergy and bishops alike. Theologians ignore her only to be ignored by the people. And throughout all this, devotion to her and interest in her message continues to grow.

What is her power? What is her compelling force? What is the logic of Guadalupe devotion which seems to defy our systems of logic and reasoning? What is the inner force that continues to make her so alive and important for us?

Ask yourself: What is the power of a precious gift given to us by someone we love?

I suspect, in a simple way, its innermost power is that it is a gift from God. Protestants tell me: "But Christ alone is necessary for salvation." And I say to them: "You are absolutely right. That is precisely what makes Guadalupe so precious. Precisely because she is not necessary, she is so special! She is a gift of God's love."

Aren't the most precious things in our lives the gifts that were given to us? They are so precious precisely because they were not necessary. How often have we told someone we love: "You don't have to give me anything!" Yet the lover insists, and we treasure the gift. Life would be so dull if it were reduced to only the absolutely necessary things in life and salvation itself would become mechanical reduced to only that which is necessary.

I suspect that is one reason why I love our popular Catholic tradition of processions, devotions, relics, candles, holy water and other sacramentals. It is the whole complex of these many "unnecessary" manifestations of God's love that allows God's love to appear so plentiful, personal and beautiful.

Recall the help of a teacher or coach, or the little extras your parents or grandparents gave you, or a friend or even a stranger who was there for you in a moment of need. Look at the many "unnecessary" things which became so important in your life. Just think what incredible power you have to bring about that richness of life within others.

The expanding power and force of Guadalupe is that it is a precious gift of God's love to the people of the Americas at the very moment it started to become the land of the great encounter of all the peoples of the world. The more we recall what she has done for us and what she continues to do today, the more devotion to her grows.

At a time when people of the old world and the new world were tearing each other apart, our Mother came to begin the healing. At a time when people were in such great pain and hopelessness that they only wanted to die, she comes to offer hope and life. At a moment of colossal birth pangs for a new people, the people of the Americas, God gives us Guadalupe as our precious birthday gift to remain with us and accompany us throughout the long pilgrimage.

Devotion to Our Lady of Guadalupe has never been mandated, like Sunday attendance at Mass, but there is no need to make it an obligation. Why mandate what people love to do? Even if the devotion were prohibited, the prohibition would be useless. The testimonies of favors granted through her continue to circulate among the faithful.

The devotion continues to spread because personal stories of her favors continue to abound. The unquestioned conviction of her miraculous power is transmitted not only by word of mouth, but by a growing consciousness that seems to transmit the devotion from generation to generation. People throughout the Americas continue to bring flowers and mementos to her as simple gestures of heartfelt gratitude.

Guadalupe was miraculously painted on the tilma of Juan Diego, but she is not just a painting, she is the living icon of God's maternal presence, the living icon of God's tender love and compassion for all the inhabitants of the Americas. She takes to her bosom all who gaze upon her in faith. It is within her womb that this beautiful Indian Mother recreates the various races, ethnic groups and religions of the Americas into the one family of her children. It is within her that divisions, borders and hatreds dissolve as we begin to see one another not as the world sees—by division and segregation—but as she sees: the beloved children of one mother, loving brothers and sisters.

Her devotion will continue to grow because she makes the love of God ever more personal and ever more present to us. At a time when people feel more and more isolated, she comes to offer a common home for all.

Her requested temple is just beginning to be built. Yes, the physical temple has been built and rebuilt, but the real temple she requested—an America for all her children—is just beginning. It will not be complete until there is an America without borders, without border patrols or immigration police, an America without homeless and abandoned children and elderly; an America with truly equal opportunities for everyone; an America where the goods of these rich lands will truly be enjoyed by everyone and not just by a privileged few.

Her temple is the common family home for all the inhabitants of this land. May we go forth from this retreat proclaiming and living that conviction as true sons and daughters of Our Lady of Guadalupe, Patroness of the Americas.

For Reflection

- *In what ways have you recognized Mary's maternal presence in your parish? In your country?*

- *Our Lady of Guadalupe elevated the social dignity of the indigenous Americans. How have you helped others to see beyond their differences? How have you helped them to esteem themselves?*

- *Consider Mary's role in bringing God to humanity in the person of Jesus. Spend some time thanking God for the good things which have been accomplished through your many ordinary "yes" responses to God.*

Closing Prayer

O Holy Mother of Guadalupe, come into my life just as you did Juan Diego's. I am grateful for your love and protection, your healing and comfort; thank you for choosing to remain among us always. I have nothing to fear in life because you, my mother, are with me always. I know that you will never abandon me and even when I forget about you, I know that you have not forgotten me. Help me to become, like Juan Diego, an ambassador of your message of love and equality for all the inhabitants of the Americas. Amen.

Deepening Your Acquaintance

To learn more about Our Lady of Guadalupe and Juan Diego, consider these resources.

Books

Elizondo, Virgilio. *La Morenita*. San Antonio: Mexican American Cultural Center, 1980.

_____. *Guadalupe: Mother of the New Creation*. Maryknoll, N.Y.: Orbis Books, 1997.

Gabriele, Edward Francis. *My Soul Magnifies the Lord*. Notre Dame, Ind.: Ave Maria Press, 1996.

Rodriguez, Jeanette. *Our Lady of Guadalupe: Faith and Empowerment Among Mexican-American Women*. Austin, Tex.: University of Texas Press, 1994.

Articles

Lucero, Robert, O.F.M. "Guadalupe and the Immaculate Conception." *St. Anthony Messenger*, December 12, 1983, pp. 18-22.

"Our Lady of Guadalupe to Juan Diego," CARA Studies on Popular Devotion, Vol. 2: *Guadalupan Studies*, Monograph No. 6.

Sandoval, Moises. "Our Lady of Guadalupe: 450 Years." *Maryknoll Magazine*, December 1981, pp. 10-14.

Videos

El Gran Acontecimiento (The Great Event). Animated story of Our Lady of Guadalupe. Available from St. Anthony Messenger Press and Franciscan Communications.

Mary: Model of Contemporary Discipleship. Presented by Rev. Virgilio Elizondo and Rev. Bertrand Buby. Part V of "Vatican II Vision 2000: The Teaching Church." Available from Sheed and Ward.

Nuestra Senora de Guadalupe (Our Lady of Guadalupe). Available from Saint Anthony Messenger Press and Franciscan Communications.

Once on a Barren Hill. Dramatization of Guadalupe story. Available from Ignatius Press.

Our Lady of Guadalupe. Dramatization of story of Juan Diego and the Lady. Available from Videos With Values.

About the Authors

VIRGILIO ELIZONDO is a diocesan priest, theologian and founder of the Mexican-American Cultural Center in San Antonio, Texas. He was awarded the 1997 Laetare Medal by the University of Notre Dame, considered the most prestigious honor given to U.S. Catholics. He is a member of the Catholic Common Ground project.

JEANETTE RODRIGUEZ is mother, wife, theologian, chair of the department of theology at Seattle University and president of the Academy of Hispanic Catholic Theologians in the United States (ACHTUS).

GLORIA INES LOYA, P.B.V.M., teaches at the Jesuit School of Theology at Berkeley, California.

ANITA de LUNA, M.C.D.P., is pursuing a Ph.D. in Hispanic spirituality at Georgetown Theological Union.

ALEX GARCIA-RIVERA is married and is a professor of systematic theology at the Jesuit School of Theology.

ROSENDO URRABAZO, C.M.F., Ph.D., earned his doctorate degree in religion and psychology from the Graduate Theological Union in Berkeley, California.